RAILS ACROSS AUSTRALIA

A JOURNEY THROUGH THE CONTINENT

RAILS ACROSS AUSTRALIA

A JOURNEY THROUGH THE CONTINENT

DAVID CABLE

PEN & SWORD
TRANSPORT

First published in Great Britain in 2015 by
Pen & Sword Transport
An imprint of Pen & Sword Books Ltd
47 Church Street
Barnsley
South Yorkshire
S70 2AS

ISBN 978 1 47384 436 0

Printed and bound by Imago Publishing Limited.

Pen & Sword Books Ltd incorporates the imprints of Pen & Sword Archaeology,
Atlas, Aviation, Battleground, Discovery, Family History, History, Maritime, Military,
Naval, Politics, Railways, Select, Social History, Transport, True Crime, and Claymore
Press, Frontline Books, Leo Cooper, Praetorian Press, Remember When, Seaforth
Publishing and Wharncliffe.

For a complete list of Pen & Sword titles please contact
Pen & Sword Books Limited
47 Church Street, Barnsley, South Yorkshire, S70 2AS, England
E-mail: enquiries@pen-and-sword.co.uk
Website: www.pen-and-sword.co.uk

DAVID CABLE – OTHER PUBLICATIONS

Railfreight in Colour (for the modeller and historian)

BR Passenger Sectors in Colour (for the modeller and historian)

Lost Liveries of Privatisation in Colour (for the modeller and historian)

Hydraulics in the West

The Blue Diesel Era

Rails across North America – A Pictorial Journey across the USA

Rails across Canada – A Pictorial Journey across Canada

Introduction

This is a book of photographs of trains that I have taken in various parts of the mainland of the Commonwealth of Australia, firstly of mainly preserved steam operations in South Australia, where I lived between 1967 and 1973, and then at the main lines in the five mainland states during nine holidays taken throughout the twenty-first century. Schedules have never allowed time to visit Tasmania or the two territories.

The comments about rolling stock are largely from my own observations of what I regard as a dynamic set of operations in a country full of fascinating and attractive locations, even if the sun didn't shine every day! The book will be primarily marketed in Australia, but also elsewhere such as the USA and UK. The text below is therefore written to provide background for those people, so I am afraid that Aussies will find it like telling your grandmother to suck eggs, but I hope they will enjoy the pictures.

The Railway Systems

The early history of Australian railways led to one of the most chaotic situations relating to transport systems anywhere in the world.

As railways started to become a reliable means of transportation, each of the original state cities on the continent employed engineers to initiate a railway system based about the city hub and into its environs, but failing to recognise that, in time, development would require links between the states and the cities.

So it was unfortunate that each engineer had his own ideas as to what track gauge to use. The net result was that only two states – Victoria and South Australia – chose a gauge that allowed straightforward interconnection, whereas at every other state boundary on the mainland, people and freight had to be unloaded and reloaded.

The individual choices were that New South Wales selected standard 4' 8 1/2" /1,435mm gauge, Victoria and South Australia the 'Irish' 5' 3"/1,600mm, and Queensland, Western Australia and parts of South Australia the 'light' 3' 6" /1,067mm version. Later-built lines, such as the link across the Nullarbor desert between SA and WA and the iron ore lines in the Pilbara region of Western Australia, have been of standard gauge.

As a result, once the original imports of locomotives and rolling stock to get each system established were up and running and the systems expanded, each of the states developed their own designs to deal with the extra requirements.

It was not until the 1960s that the decision was made that the state capitals should all be connected by one standard gauge track system, and to be able to generate standard locomotives and rolling stock to operate throughout the new lines. These have now been enhanced by the line through Alice Springs to Darwin, and the short branch from Port Augusta to the steel-

The complications of different track widths are exemplified by this old triple gauge turnout at Gladstone SA. (DC Collection)

producing town of Whyalla in South Australia.

However, most of the original lines are still extant and often well used. For example, in Queensland, the state capital Brisbane is close to the state border, so that the standard gauge from New South Wales hardly penetrates the state, which therefore still uses the original 3' 6" /1,067mm lines. In Western Australia, the narrow gauge tracks still carry almost all traffic around Perth and the south western parts of the state. Suburban and country lines in Victoria are broad gauge operated, and there is still one broad gauge branch in South Australia, plus the remote narrow gauge system based on Port Lincoln. So it is only in New South Wales where the interstate and intrastate operations are fully integrated.

In establishing the systems as they developed, what might be called the standard British Empire methods of track laying were used. To be as economical as possible, these were based on following the contours of the land with the minimum of engineering works in terms of cuttings, embankments, tunnels and viaducts, level crossings providing access for road vehicles and animal stock. Single tracks with occasional passing loops provided sufficient capacity outside of conurbations, although with the passage of time, widening these to double tracks became necessary as traffic grew. And between Newcastle and Maitland in New South Wales, traffic is now of a density to require four tracks.

What is, perhaps, surprising is that in spite of the very few overbridges and tunnels, the loading gauge still restricts the use of double-stacked containers as widely used in North America, apart from between Adelaide and Perth, even though the cost of enlarging them would be relatively small, and would give a substantial increase in some line capacity.

The infrastructure is quite varied, with lightly laid narrow gauge tracks with limited axle loadings in some of the remoter country areas, up to heavy rail, deep ballasted lines for the interstate and heavy haulage operations.

The Railway Companies

In the first years, the railways were owned and operated by their respective states, plus Commonwealth Railways, which built the line from Port Augusta to Kalgoorlie across the Nullarbor desert. But over time various mergers took place, sectorisation developed and private companies began to gain access to the main lines. The major players in more recent times comprise:

New South Wales Government Railways, which operate CountryLink and CityLink passenger trains. Their freight train operations were sectorised into Freight Corporation (FreightCorp), now part of Pacific National (Pac Nat).

Victoria Railways (V-Rail), which operates all passenger services in the state, including Melbourne Metro services. Freight operations were separated to form Freight Victoria, later Freight Australia, now also part of Pac Nat.

Queensland Rail runs all passenger and freight services in that state, but has developed into QR National, which now runs freight trains on standard gauge tracks between the state capitals and Hunter Valley coal trains. The company has been rebranded Aurizon.

South Australian Railways merged with Commonwealth Railways to form Australia National, which was taken over by the

American company, Genesee & Wyoming, using the brand name Australian Southern, and later Australian Rail Group (ARG) after it acquired freight operations in Western Australia. SAR in embryo form still operates the Adelaide metro trains.

Western Australia Government Railways now operates all passenger services on the narrow gauge lines in WA. Freight operations are handled by ARG and Pac Nat.

Tasmanian Government Railways (outside the ambit of this book).

National Rail was established when the standard gauge network was developed between the states, but freight activities have been absorbed by Pac Nat, and long-distance passenger trains are run privately (see below).

Pac Nat operates freight services on all the standard gauge lines, plus certain intermodal services on the narrow gauge main line in Queensland, apart from trains in the Pilbara area of WA.

Pilbara Rail (formerly Hamersley Iron and Robe River) and BHP Billiton (formerly Mount Newman and Goldsworthy Mining) have remote operations handling iron ore for export. They are both situated in the Pilbara area in the north west of the continent.

CFCLA (Chicago Freight Leasing Company of America) is a company which leases locomotives and other rolling stock to various operators.

There are also several smaller private companies who operate both nationally or locally, some of which seem to be on a shoestring budget and don't last long. Of these the more prominent are Specialised Container Transport (SCT), which runs trains from Melbourne to Perth, FreightLink (now part of Pac Nat), which ran freight trains from Adelaide to Darwin, and Xstrata, one of the major coal carrying companies in the Hunter Valley of NSW. Also worthy of mention is West Coast Railways, now defunct, which operated passenger services between Melbourne and Geelong/Warnamboul.

The present day trains
Passenger services

Passenger services fall into three categories.

Interstate trains are operated by Great Southern Rail, and in one case by New South Wales Government Railways and Victorian Railways. These comprise the Indian Pacific to and from Sydney and Perth via Adelaide, the Overland to and from Adelaide and Melbourne, and the Ghan to and from Adelaide and Darwin, plus the NSW/VR service between Sydney and Melbourne. With the exception of the latter train, which runs twice daily, the other three operate on only two or three days per week. The Indian Pacific, Overland and Ghan are normally hauled by NR class locomotives, sometimes with assistance from another class. The Sydney/Melbourne service is worked by XPT diesel multiple units.

Intrastate services are run centred on the state capitals, most running on a daily out and return basis, although some are on a twice per day basis, such as from Sydney to Canberra. In Victoria many are more frequent and are of relatively short distances. In Queensland, along the coast services are generally daily, but to the more remote inland areas are less frequent. Western Australia run some services daily, others on a more occasional basis, whilst South Australia have no intrastate services at all. New South Wales trains comprise services operated by XPT units over the longer distances, including just over the state border into Brisbane, and Explorer DMUs for most other services. These are operated under the title CountryLink. In Victoria, V-Line work the services, most of which are worked by that organisation's broad gauge locomotives, although DMUs are now encroaching especially with trains to the Geelong area. Queensland trains use their own system's narrow gauge locomotives, with the exception of the City of Rockhampton trains, which are electric tilting train units. Western Australia uses DMUs for all its interstate trains.

Suburban services, with one exception, are based around the

state capital cities, and vary in intensity. In Sydney and Melbourne, electric trains provide a very frequent range of train services, both within and to the outlying parts of the areas using modern rolling stock. Brisbane is similar, but without the intensity of the other two, whilst Perth and Adelaide's trains have been somewhat more infrequent, probably reflecting the lower populations. Adelaide's diesel multiple units are now being replaced by electric trains. The exception is the Hunter Valley service from Newcastle to Telarah, near Maitland, and occasionally to Muswellbrook, the main service running at a twice per hour interval throughout the middle of the day, and more often in the rush hours. This pattern is typical of all such lines. All trains, in my experience, are well patronised. The trains themselves are all multiple units to the designs of each state's own requirements, double-deck trains being the standard for Sydney, classified as CityLink.

Freight trains

Freight trains carry several major 'products' plus a limited number of other loads. The biggest items are bulk minerals (iron ore, coal, limestone, cement), international type containers and grain. Other items include steel sections, livestock (now only in Queensland), liquid fuels, containerised mineral concentrates, ballast and other infrastructure items, and other service requirements such as local fuels and liquids. Some of these are seasonal items, but the majority run throughout the year.

The most outstanding trains are first and foremost, the trains carrying iron ore for export, which work on the two systems in the Pilbara. These trains carry pay loads of at least 20,000 tons of ore, and in the case of BHP Billiton even as much as 30,000 tons on some services. The BHP trains operate with multiple locos on the front and mid-train, whereas Pilbara Rail use two locos on the front, having been assisted by rear end helpers when leaving the mines.

Next are the coal trains of the Hunter Valley in NSW and the Blackwater and Goonyella lines in Queensland. These all load to around 10,000 tons per train, and operate a very high volume of services throughout the year. All of this coal is for export. Hunter Valley trains are diesel hauled with multiple locos on the front end, whilst the Queensland operations are electrified, with trains having mid-train helpers. Both the iron ore and coal trains use bogie wagons with tare load capacity of around 100 tons.

Intermodal services run between the state capitals and a few other towns. These are operated by Pacific National using NR class locos (see below), but are normally single stacked, with a very few which can be twin stacked between Adelaide and Perth.

Locomotives

From the early days, steam locomotives were imported from the UK, but in time the state railways built their own workshops and manufactured their own designs for their own gauges. Early dieselisation also provided for some imports, but the majority of diesels have been built in the Commonwealth either under licence from US companies, or have been to their own designs, but fitted with US diesel engines (EMD, GE and Alco). These designs have generally ranged up to around 3,000 horse power/2,240kW, which was normally sufficient for intrastate use.

But with the coming of the standard gauge network, and the development of the mineral export systems, higher output locomotives became necessary. Initially, second generation locos up to 3,800HP/2,860kW were introduced such as the 90 class for FreightCorp, the G and BL classes for Freight Victoria and Australian National, and the 4,000 class for QR. However these were not available or suitable for nationwide use.

Therefore, third generation engines were becoming a necessity and the NR class was introduced from the mid-1990s to operate intermodal and long-distance passenger trains. These 4,000HP/3,000kW engines becoming the largest class to operate in Australia. These were built with General Electric diesel power. These have been augmented by designs particularly for the coal traffic, with local designs of diesel locomotives of up to 4,300HP/3,200kW.

But more recently, and particularly in the Pilbara area, locomotives have been imported, especially from North America, and now a few from China. The locomotives in the Pilbara are standard US designs from GE and EMD. For FreightCorp/Pac Nat, engines were built by EMD in Canada to an Australian specification.

The new electric locomotives on the coal lines in Queensland have been built to Australian designs by Siemens in Germany, with some rebuilt locally using Siemens equipment.

However, many of the older designs are still extant, being used both by the individual states and by some of the smaller operators. New designs are being introduced, so that the range and variety of locomotives seen in the country is quite stimulating.

Not to be forgotten are the power cars of the XPT. These trains are based on the InterCity 125 trains introduced by British Rail in the mid-1970s, with a 2,000HP/1,500kW diesel engined power car at each end of the train set. Track layouts inhibit their ability to meet the 125mph operating speed of the British version, but they nevertheless provide fast services based from Sydney.

The diesel powered locomotives were built by several manufacturers. The Alco powered engines were mainly built by A.E. Goodwin; EMD powered locos by Clyde, now EDI Rail, who have factories in several locations; and GE powered units by Goninan, now United Group based in Broadmeadow, Newcastle. In the early days, a number of designs were manufactured by English Electric and then by a local subsidiary in Australia. Electric locomotives were built by Comeng and Walkers, with the newest design in Queensland built by Krauss Maffei in Germany.

A number of locomotives are named, some with cast nameplates, but most with adhesive-backed 'labels'. Names cover locations, personages and aboriginal descriptions, but only the V-Line N class, G&W CLP class and FQ class carry names on every class member. A little over half of the 120 NR class carry the adhesive labels.

Summary

The purpose of this book is to give an outsider's view into what can be seen in many parts of Australia, and how things are developing in this part of the world.

It also makes me some money!

The pictures are all of my own taking. Some locations have been visited several times. The four track Hunter Valley line between Warabrook and Maitland carries a great deal of traffic. The station areas provide good facilities for photographs so travelling by local trains saves the cost of car hire. Dry Creek has a road between the main line and the loco shed, so that there are fairly frequent train movements taking place, especially on a Saturday.

The early steam photographs are not of prime quality, having been taken on some unknown film of dubious characteristics, but are included because of their historical interest.

My travels have given me only a small view of this vast country, full of interest and some super people. I have been helped by finding locations shown in magazines, in particular the top-class bi-monthly publication *Motive Power*. I want to give special thanks to certain persons associated with the magazine who have taken me around and given me advice – Chris Nuthall, Stuart Ellis, Peter Attenborough and Bruce Russell. I have also made substantial use of Peter Clark's book *An Australian Locomotive Guide* in providing details of the different engine classes.

Since my younger daughter and family now live in Brisbane, I need no excuse for not being able to pay many more visits to Oz in the years to come, and add more photos in more locations to the collection.

David Cable
Hartley Wintney, Hants, UK
December 2014

1967-1973

SAR class Rx 4-6-0 No. 207 passes through Belair station with an ARHS special train from Adelaide to Aldgate, c1968. This class was introduced in 1899 and built at the South Australian Railway workshops at Islington.

SAR 4-8-4 No. 526 *Duchess of Gloucester* makes the echoes ring as it storms through Eden Hills with an ARHS special, on the climb up to the summit of the Adelaide Hills at Mount Lofty, c1969. These locomotives are styled on the Pennsylvania RR T1 class of 4-4-4-4 engines, and were built at Islington in 1943.

The historic meeting at Port Pirie SA, when SAR 4-8-4 No. 526 *Duchess of Gloucester* posed alongside NSWGR class C38 4-6-2 No. 3813 in 1969, when 3813 had worked with its sister locomotive 3801 on the first steam hauled trans-continental train from Sydney to Perth. Engine 3801 carried on by itself from Port Pirie. The two locomotives were, of course, of different gauges.

NSWGR C38 Pacific 3813 is seen near Port Germein SA in 1969, running a special from Port Pirie to Port Augusta in conjunction with the trans-continental celebration. The pride of the NSWGR passenger fleet, they were built by Clyde from 1942.

Following its return to service, SAR 4-8-4 520 *Sir Malcolm Barclay* is seen leaving Adelaide station in pristine condition, with a special to Aldgate in 1970.

A pair of SAR Alco 'World' type DL500 diesels with an English Electric class 900 are seen near Elizabeth SA in 1971, with a southbound freight train probably destined for the yards at Mile End, Adelaide. This photo was taken whilst waiting for a northbound special working. These 1,600HP/1,190kW locos were fitted with Alco 251 diesel engines, and built under licence by A.E. Goodwin.

What was promoted as a steam special working going north from Adelaide, turned out to be this pair of vintage railcars, seen near Elizabeth. A disappointment at the time but in retrospect, quite interesting.

Commonwealth Railways GM 42 heads the empty stock of the train that had taken the Prime Minister, Gough Whitlam, to open the line from Port Augusta to Whyalla SA in 1972. The train is passing through the nicely kept station at Port Augusta. Built from 1955 by Clyde, they are fitted with 1,800HP/1,340kW EMD 567 diesels.

A steam hauled special from Sydney travelled to Whyalla to help celebrate the opening of the line from Port Augusta in 1972. The train was hauled by NSWGR C38 4-6-2 3801 (as far as Port Augusta) and C36 4-6-0 3672, seen here at Whyalla being watered in a mini dust storm created by the wind blowing down the newly laid ballast. This class dates from 1925, when they were built by Clyde.

SAR light Pacific 621 *Duke of Edinburgh* gives all its worth as it passes the attractive station at Eden Hills SA with an ARHS special in 1973. These locos were built at Islington by SAR in 1936.

A pair of Hamersley Iron C636s, 2017 leading, wait outside Dampier WA for their trainload of iron ore to be unloaded at the palletising plant in 1971. Another train waits in the distance. These 3,600HP/2,680kW engines, powered by Alco 251 diesels, were built by A.E. Goodwin.

1983-2000

A pair of NSWGR JT26C-255 class 81s, 8105 and 8107, head towards the Newcastle area with a Hunter Valley coal train, seen near Hexham NSW in March 1983. With 3,000HP/2,240kW power, they were introduced by Clyde in 1982. (DC Collection)

On the main line running north to Brisbane, four NSWGR 44204, 4461, 4451 and 4464 Alcos haul a well-loaded intermodal service past Loadstone NSW in October 1992. Both classes were powered by Alco 251 diesels of 2,000HP/1,490kW and 1,800HP/1,340kW respectively, all being built by Goodwins. (DC Collection)

V Line P21 waits to depart from Flinders Street station, Melbourne, with a passenger service in November 1992, whilst T 390 hides its nose in a van. The P class were rebuilt from the T class with 1,000HP/746kW EMD 567 diesels, replacing the T class engines of 875HP/650kW. Both classes were built by Clyde. (DC Collection)

With the clock tower at Sydney Central station standing proud, Freight Corp J26C class 42209 stands at the head of the stock of the Indian Pacific in November 1992. The 422 class was of 2,000HP/1,490kW power from an EMD 645 diesel, and were built by Clyde. (DC Collection)

A very smart line up at Lithgow NSW in November 1992. From left to right, NSWGR CE615 class 8015, Freight Corp DL531 class 48115 and NSWGR 8047. 8015 is in the Candy Stripe colour scheme, 8047 being in the Tuscan Red scheme. Both classes have Alco 251 diesels, the 80 class being of 2,000HP/1,490kW and built by Comeng from 1978, the 48 class being 950HP/670kW and built by Goodwins from 1966. (DC Collection)

A line up of CL627 class 85 electric locos at Lithgow, with 8502 in the Tuscan Red colour scheme at the head. These 1979 built 3,850HP/2,880kW locos have the same output as the 1983 built class 86, both classes having been constructed by Comeng using Mitsubishi electrical equipment. (DC Collection)

In mixed NSWGR colours, a pair of Alco DL500 class 44s led by 4467 pass Paterson NSW with a freight train in November 1992. (DC Collection)

Queensland Rail 1620 stands outside the shed at Mayne in the Brisbane suburbs in November 1992. Built under licence from English Electric, these locos only had an output of 860HP/640kW. They were introduced in 1967. (DC Collection)

WAGR MA class 1862 and D class 1561 stand with departmental wagons in the yard at Forrestfield WA. The MA class of three locos were diesel hydraulic shunters using a Caterpillar diesel of 700HP/520kW. The five D class were 2,000HP/1,490kW locos with EMD 645 diesels, built by Clyde in 1971. (DC Collection)

AT Perth Terminal (now East Perth Terminal) WAGR LGT26C class 256 waits patiently, while passengers disembark from the train in November 1992. This 3,000HP/2,240kW class looks very similar to the US SD40s; they use EMD 645 diesels, and were built by Clyde in 1967. (DC Collection)

A CityLink service heads south towards Wynyard and Central station as it leaves Sydney Harbour Bridge. Seen on the way down off the bridge in February 2000. (Jim Osborne)

A grain train heads south through Bundanoon, splitting the semaphores in June 2000. The lead loco, L254, is in the now obsolete ATN Access colours, and is followed by EL51 in AN colours. The CM30-8 EL class use General Electric 7FDL diesels of 3,200HP/2,380kW and were built by Goninan in 1990. (DC Collection)

2001
Sydney CityLink EMU C3605 draws to a halt at Circular Quay with a train bound for Liverpool. Above the station is a highway link to the Harbour Bridge, the harbour and quays being to the left of the picture, April 2001.

Last days of the mainline electric locos. FreightCorp 8609 and 8617 pass through Lidcombe with an intermodal service heading for the docks in April 2001.

A CityLink service worked by EMU V10 heads west through Auburn in the western suburbs of Sydney.

Spectators on the platform watch as the Indian Pacific gets going on its journey across the continent, seen here passing Auburn NSW, with National Rail's NR 104 taking the strain. The NR locos were introduced in 1996, built by Goninan with GE 7FDL diesels. They are classed Cv40-9i and the 120-strong fleet is the largest class in Australia.

NSWGR CityLink DMU 621 stops at Warabrook on the outskirts of Newcastle, with a Telarah to Newcastle stopping service. These units appealed to me, with their air conditioning systems of a bulkhead in the centre of the coach fitted with a small fan and a gas fire! Of course, one could also open the windows on a hot day, when the fan couldn't cope!

Three FreightCorp Alcos, 48156, 48120 and 48153, pass Warabrook with a westbound grain train. These little locos always appealed to me, and would be perfect for a model railway layout.

The big beasts of FreightCorp were (and still are) the EMD built class 90s, two of which, 9006 and 9013, are seen passing Warabrook with a coal train scheduled for Port Waratah. Fitted with 3,850HP/2,860kW EMD 710 diesels, they were built by EMD in Canada from 1994.

The daily intermodal service from Sandgate to Sydney passes Warabrook behind ANR liveried EL56, with Great Northern GMs 27 and 22. Regrettably, vandals had got at No. 22 in Sydney over the Easter weekend, ruining the photo of the train when it went up to Sandgate.

A CountryLink Explorer class DMU accelerates away from Sandgate, with a Newcastle to Telarah stopping service. This view has changed substantially since this photo was taken in April 2001, now that a flyover for coal trains destined for Kooragang Island has been installed.

FreightCorp 9025, 9027 and 9016 negotiate the dip between Beresfield and Thornton with a train of empties returning to one of the Hunter Valley coal mines in April 2001.

The coal empties are followed through Thornton NSW by FreightCorp class 48 Alcos 48154/115/125/128 with a train of grain empties.

Noted as a Brisbane to Melbourne intermodal (which may be in some doubt), NR 51 heads a short train over the junction at Thornton, with the hump between here and Metford being left behind.

XPT power car 2001 was painted in special colours to commemorate the centenary of the establishment of the Commonwealth of Australia in 1901. The striking livery catches the eye as it passes Thornton with a Sydney to Armidale service.

More Hunter Valley coal bound for the Newcastle area behind FreightCorp 9012, 9020 and 9015 with its train snaking back over the summit as it takes the back road past Thornton station.

Making a change from the normal motive power seen on the Hunter Valley lines, FreightCorp 8121 passes Thornton with a northbound train of ore concentrate containers.

A shot showing the layout of Thornton station and track layout as it was in April 2001, and also including FreightCorp Alcos 48123, 48164, 48145 and 48160 with a southbound grain train.

In the attractive old passenger livery of Australian National, CLP10 *Mirning* passes the day on shed at Dry Creek SA in April 2001. Originally built in 1970 by Clyde with an EMD 645 diesel, they were upgraded by Morrison Knudsen at Whyalla in 1993 to provide 3,300HP/2,460kW with head end power so as to be able to work the Indian Pacific and Ghan passenger trains.

ANR 508 is parked at the back of Dry Creek shed with what I assume is a departmental coach. Although not marked, Australia Southern had by this time taken over from ANR. Built at Islington in 1964, they have 500HP/375kW English Electric diesels.

Ex-Australian National 607 stands in Dry Creek shed in front of another Alco, this time of class 700. Also taken over by AS, these DL541 class of Alco 1,800HP/1,340kW engined locos were built in 1965 by A.E. Goodwin.

Showing the Australia Southern logo, but still in ANR colours, Alco 844 looks rather shabby as it stands in the yard outside Dry Creek shed.

In the full colours of owners Genesee & Wyoming Industries, Australia Southern CLP 11 and CLP 8 pause at Dry Creek with a Melbourne to Perth intermodal. Note the coach for the relief crew used during the long journey to Western Australia, and the double-stack container, a facility used west of Adelaide where no tunnel or bridge restrictions occur. The locomotives are named *Kaurna* and *City of Port Augusta* respectively.

ANR coloured, AS labelled Alco 705 comes out from under the main highway at Dry Creek with an Adelaide bound intermodal working. These were a larger version of the 600 series locos, with a 2,000HP/1,490kW engine. They were built in 1971, and were similar to the NSWGR class 442.

Australia Southern GM 44 leads GM 46 in ANR livery with a grain train passing Dry Creek.

National Rail NR 44 passes Dry Creek with the eastbound Indian Pacific from Perth to Sydney via Adelaide in April 2001.

An interesting combination of AS DA2, CK4 and 841 shunt a short freight train at Dry Creek. The DA class were cut-down hood versions of the SAR 830 class (similar to the FreightCorp 48 class). The CK class were originally V-Line T class locos.

Trans Adelaide DMUs 3001 and 3020, which sports Smart Move advertisements, pass Dry Creek on their way from Gawler to Adelaide.

Stabled in the intermodal terminal at Islington SA, NR 52 shows off its aboriginal based colour scheme, albeit not quite in the best of condition.

A preserved SAR Bluebird DMU stands in the yard at Islington works in April 2001

BL 35 shows off the full scale National Rail colours originally used on some locos as it stands in Islington works yard. This class is virtually the same as the 81 class, with minor detail differences.

NSWGR 42208, in rather shabby candy stripe colours, sits in the workshops at Islington, ready to be overhauled and repainted into FreightCorp livery.

J class Great Northern shunter 103 stands waiting for business at Keswick station, Adelaide, in April 2001. Built by Clyde in 1966, this class has a 600HP/445kW EMD 567 diesel engine.

The morning sun glints on the rolling stock of the Overland, which is shortly due to leave Keswick for Melbourne, behind NR 93.

Trans Adelaide DMU pair 3013 and 3016 descend the Adelaide Hills with a Belair to Adelaide service, seen entering Mitcham station in April 2001.

2003

CountryLink power car 2001 brightens the day at Spencer Street station, Melbourne (now renamed Southern Cross), in its special livery celebrating the Centenary of the Federation of the Commonwealth of Australia in 1901. It is about to depart for Sydney in April 2003.

A Connex EMU 694M heads away from Spencer Street with a Loop Line service. Connex seemed to get everywhere in those days!

West Coast Railway B65 stands at Dynon Loco Shed in Melbourne, but only carries an 'economy' version of the company's full colour scheme, as seen further on page 87. Classed ML-2, these double-cabbed 'Bulldog' styled locos were built in 1952 by Clyde and fitted with a 1,500HP/1,120kW EMD 567 diesel engine.

Great Northern T381 passes the day with one of its brothers at Dynon.

Freight Australia H5 shows off the livery, with stripes of substantial proportions for this nice little engine. These locos are similar to the T class.

I always liked the American-style look of the Victorian X class, and X37 shows its design off nicely. But only the Victorians could give themselves unwarranted status as the distorted map of the state, superimposed on the continent, shows in the obsolete Freight Victoria livery! These Clyde built engines were introduced in 1966 with EMD 567 type diesels of 1,800HP/1,340kW.

I felt fortunate to find this one-off beast on shed at Dynon, V544 *Tim Fischer*, which is a replacement for a withdrawn G class loco, and usually found in South Australia on coal trains serving Leigh Creek. EDI Rail constructed it in 2002, classified as GT46C with a 3,850HP/2,860kW EMD 710 diesel, April 2003.

Dynon shed was full of locos in classes new to me, and P19 is another example with its Freight Australia colours.

X38 was one of the first X class to be rebuilt with G class diesel engines, enlarged radiators and enlarged cabs, plus a toilet at the rear end. It has subsequently been renumbered XR550. It is seen here at Dynon in April 2003.

C508 runs light engine past a line of auto racks at Dynon, in a very orangey version of the standard National Rail colours of charcoal and apricot. It must be over ripe! The GT26CW class was built by Clyde in 1977 with EMD 3,000HP/2,240kW 645 engines.

Being prepared for future duties, RTS L265 stands in one of the workshops at Dynon, with a National Rail BL class behind.

M-train 455M passes Sunshine with a Sydenham to Flinders Street service in April 2003.

Freight Australia G511 and X52 bring a train of grain hoppers into the loop at Sunshine, before running round and returning from whence they came. Playing trains perhaps?! The G class are similar to the 81 and BL classes designated JT26C, and introduced by Clyde in 1984.

In full V-Line livery, P15 storms past Middle Footscray with what was recorded as a Melbourne to Ballarat working in April 2003.

V-Line A70 is nearly ready to leave Spencer Street station with a train bound for Seymour. Note the dual gauge track. The A class were rebuilds of the B class, using higher output EMD 645 diesels of 2,250HP/1,680kW. They were introduced in 1984, with Clyde undertaking the reconstruction.

V-Line Y129 shunts *Club Car Victoria* across the points outside Spencer Street station. This 600HP/445kW class was built by Clyde in 1963, using an EMD 567 engine.

M-train 541M arrives at North Melbourne with a Flinders Street to Sydenham service.

Showing the full effect of the adopted colours of the American Fallen Flag railroad Gulf, Mobile & Ohio, Great Northern S317 and GM10 are parked in a yard near Dynon. Both these classes were introduced in the 1950s by Clyde using EMD 567 engines generating 1,750HP/1,300kW.

In the SteelLink sector version of National Rail, NR 60 poses at South Dynon in April 2003. Not the most inspiring colours.

West Coast Railways S300 shows the full colour scheme of this owner, as it stands in Spencer Street station awaiting the green signal to herald its departure for Warrnambool.

Flinders Street station in Melbourne was at one time the busiest station in the British Empire, even exceeding Clapham Junction in London (and having spent many hours there, I find it hard to believe). Hitachi built EMU 233M leaves the station bound for Cranbourne.

Freight Australia A77 climbs the bank past Middle Footscray with a train of grain hoppers. Note that according to the map on the front end, Tasmania has sunk!

National Rail NR86 and SteelLink NR60 climb past Middle Footscray with a South Dynon to Brisbane intermodal service in April 2003.

If you are going to stay in Melbourne, you can't find a better hotel than this one on Spencer Street, where my room on the nineth floor, gave me this spectacular view over the throat of the station, where an XPT departs for Sydney.

Freight Australia G529, 523 and 543 take the freight avoiding lines behind Keswick station, Adelaide, with an intermodal service to Dimboola in April 2003.

2005

Southern Shorthaul GM 22 and GM 27 pass Canterbury NSW on their way to the docks in Sydney with an intermodal service in April 2005.

Having been kicked out from the last location for trespassing (we went there because the sun was on the right side!), in crossing the bridge to get onto the station, Australian Railroad Group (a GWI subsidiary) L3102 and L3101 passed underneath with a grain train to Port Botany.

CityLink Tangara set T+30 leaves Canterbury on its way from Sydney to Liverpool NSW.

Three CFCLA GL class, GL112/111/103, pass Canterbury on their way to the docks with an eastbound intermodal train. These locos are rebuilds of the former NSWGR 442 DL 500G engines, which had Alco 251 diesels. The rebuilds are equipped with GE 7FDL diesels of 3,200HP/2,380kW.

CFCLA EL 52 and EL53 crawl through Lidcombe with another docks-bound intermodal train.

ARG 2203, 2214 and 2201 speed through Moss Vale NSW with a northbound train of grain wagons. These locos are rebranded ex-NSWGR 422 class engines.

SteelLink liveried NR 50 and National Rail NR 93 head south past Moss Vale with southbound steel empties. The signals show a pleasing mix of colour lights and semaphores.

Ex-Freight Australia, now relabelled for QR National X54 and CFCLA EL 60, lead a Melbourne to Brisbane intermodal service past Moss Vale.

Rail Infrastructure Alco 4827 and CFCLA KL 80 head south past Moss Vale with a train of bolsters.

In what was then the new Pacific National colours, 8180 and NR 73 come to a halt at Moss Vale with a trainload of lime for Wollongong in April 2005.

A final shot at Moss Vale, taken in order to show the signal box, shows FreightCorp 8154 and 8148 polluting the atmosphere with a northbound train of lime stone. Passengers wait for the next service from Canberra to Sydney.

FreightCorp 8153, 48100 and 4898 make a change from the previous four Alco lash-up for grain empties on the line past Thornton. This photo was taken one afternoon in April 2005.

Four FreightCorp class 48s, 48110, 4874, 4889 and 48138, catch the glint of the sun as they pass the rebuilt Thornton station with a loaded grain train.

JL404, in the colours of R & H Transport Services, leads CFCLA JL402 and ex-AN GM40 past Warabrook with the daily Sandgate to Port Botany intermodal service. The JL class were previously 442 class locos, and were then rebuilt as GL class engines.

South Spur D47 and ARG 602 pass East Maitland NSW with a Broadmeadow to Martins Creek departmental working of ballast in April 2005.

CityLink DMU 731 starts away from the station East Maitland on its way from Newcastle to Telarah.

In standard National Rail charcoal and apricot, three NR class, NR 111, NR1 and NR38, speed past East Maitland with a Sydney to Brisbane intermodal train.

The classic view at East Maitland portrays a Newcastle-bound coal train rounding the curve behind FreightCorp 9012 and 9017. The number 14 in the white square on the front of the loco refers to the wagon set, and is not a train number, so that it does not indicate whether the train will unload at Kooragang Island or Port Waratah.

We return to Warabrook as dusk is falling, giving everything an orange tinge, where FreightCorp 9019 and 9025 pass the station with yet one more load of coal.

This picture of a Sydney to Fassifern EMU numbered V9 at Morriset (unable to run through to Newcastle due to engineering work and thus giving us the 'benefit' of non-air-conditioned bustitution!) is relatively incidental, compared with the superb signal on the right, April 2005.

The famous broad gauge *Stonie* from Penrice to Port Adelaide passes Dry Creek in April 2005, behind ARG 704 and 904 with a well-loaded train of colourful wagons.

The AT 42C DL class was introduced by Clyde in 1988, using the new 710 EMD diesel with an output of just over 3,000HP/2,260kW. In full National Rail regalia, DL 44 stands patiently at Dry Creek shed. I always thought the front end treatment made this a rather ugly class, however efficient they may have been.

The afternoon intermodal departure from Adelaide to Darwin passes Dry Creek behind FreightLink FQ04 and ARG CLP16 *Murunitja,* with the crew car behind the locos. FQ04 is in the least colourful livery of the class. This class of four engines all carried aboriginal names, this engine being *Aboriginal Stockman.* They were introduced in 2003 to work the newly opened extended line to Darwin from Alice Springs. Classed GT46C, they were fitted with EMD 710 diesels of 3,830HP/2,860kW, and were built by EDI Rail.

The FreightCorp PL class were rebuilds of class 48s and fitted with a remote control to operate shuttle services. However, PL1 was allocated to be the shunter at Adelaide's Keswick passenger station. It is seen in April 2005.

The Adelaide parklands host an intermodal service from Melbourne on its way to Islington terminal behind three National Rail locomotives of three different classes, namely NR 85, AN 5 and BL31. It will eventually arrive in Perth.

A portrait shot for model makers of National Rail's AN2 on Dry Creek shed. Built in 1992 by Clyde, these rather stylish locos carry a 710 EMD diesel of 3,850HP/2,860kW.

FreightLink FQ02 carries a full indigenous colour scheme as it waits to depart from Dry Creek shed with the accompanying crew coach for its next call of duty. This loco was named *Purnu*. April 2005.

A Perth to Melbourne intermodal passes Dry Creek shed behind three National Rail NR class locos, but in three different colour variations. In standard National Rail charcoal and apricot NR28 leads, followed by Ghan liveried NR 109 and tailed by SteelLink NR58.

The eastbound *Indian Pacific* heads for Adelaide and finally Sydney as it passes Virginia SA in April 2005, behind NR15 and DL45, splitting the grove of gum trees. The autorack behind the locos appears to be earning its keep.

The sun stayed just above the horizon long enough to be able to photograph the Ghan leaving Keswick terminal for Darwin behind a matched pair of Ghan liveried locos, NR109 and NR74, in April 2005.

The evening rush hour is starting at Perth main station, from where Transperth EMU 342 will soon be departing.

The buildings of Perth almost overwhelm Trans WA ADP103 DMU, which is working the *Australind* from Perth to Bunbury. It is seen passing McIver WA in April 2005.

WAGR P2010 and P2002 haul an eastbound grain train past Woodbridge WA. This station is just west of Midland. Note the different colours of the two locomotives. Classed GM25-8, they have GE 7FDL diesels of 2,450HP/1,830kW, and were introduced by Goninan in 1990.

Specialised Container Transport's H5, seen running light engine at Woodbridge, was one of a class of five engines fitted with an English Electric diesel of 860HP/640kW. They date from 1965.

Prospector DMU WDA001 speeds past Woodbridge on a test run in April 2001. Note the fancy colour scheme.

Transperth EMU 338 waits to leave the terminus at Fremantle for Midland. A clean design of train at a smart station.

In the words of the old adage 'Let the train take the strain', and what better illustration of it than in this view at Glendalough WA, where Transperth EMU 224 moves effortlessly along the central reservation with a service from Perth to Whitfords in the evening rush hour in April 2005.

Ex-Robe River, now Pilbara Rail, C636 9416, built under licence from Alco by Goodwins, stands at Seven Mile WA, the location of the Hamersley Iron/Pilbara Rail workshops, in April 2005. Note the air intercooler to reduce the temperture of hot intake air suffered in this part of Australia. What a beast of an engine!

Pilbara Rail C44-9W 7076, labelled for Hamersley Iron, stands outside the shops at Seven Mile. All the locos of this class were built by General Electric at Erie PA in the USA, being examples of a very large standard class used by the major railroads in North America. Their diesel engines produce 4,400HP/3,270kW.

Ex-Robe River CM40-8M 9420 and 9417, built by Goninan in 1989, with GE 7FDL diesel engines of 4,000HP/2,980kW, are parked at Seven Mile. Note the Pilbara style cab front designed to minimise the heat of the sun on the cab's front windows.

Hamersley Iron C36-7 5051 and 5052 are ready to leave Seven Mile with a transfer load of iron ore for Dampier processing plant. Alongside are ex-Robe River CM40-8M 9419 and 9425. The C36-7 engines are fitted with GE 7FDL diesels with an output of 3,750HP/2,800kW, and were built by Goninan in 1987.

Hamersley Iron C44-9Ws 7068 and 7081 pass Brolga-Dingo WA with one of the huge trains of iron ore bound for Dampier, where the ore will be processed and exported.

A pair of C44-9Ws return to the mine with a trainload of empty ore wagons passing Brolga-Dingo. In the lead is Hamersley Iron liveried 7069 with Pilbara Rail 9401, labelled for Robe River.

The full length of one of the Pilbara rail ore trains, 224 wagons each with a 100-ton capacity, is seen approaching Seven Mile behind Pilbara Rail (Robe River labelled) C44-9Ws 9406 and 9430 in April 2005.

The 'moonscape' of rocky outcrops surround Pilbara Rail C44-9Ws 7064 and 9428 as they approach Dampier with another train of iron ore to be unloaded at Parker Point.

The crossing lights of Highway I flash as C44-0W 9409 passes with a service train of tank wagons, which has left Dampier for the inland areas. This was taken as the sun was starting to set in April 2005.

A pair of BHP iron ore empties wait to depart from Port Hedland WA, watched over by a pelican, whose beak appears to be holding less than his belly can! In the foreground train, a pair of CM40-8M locos, 5667 and 5630, show off the BHP Iron Ore blue colours and the newer BHPBIO colours of the landscape. Loco 5662 heads the train behind. This class is similar to the Robe River 9400 class seen earlier.

BHPBIO CW60AC 6076, SD40 3089 and BHP CW60AC 6073 wait for business in Port Hedland yards. Engine 6076 is named *Mount Goldsworthy* and 6073 *Fortescue*. The SD40 is one of several ex-Southern Pacific locos imported to help out an engine shortage, the units having been overhauled in Mexico before shipment. The CW60ACs 6,000HP/4,480kW locos had GE 7HDL diesels and were built in 1998 by General Electric in Erie PA, being a standard US design.

Having now picked up a load, the three engines are seen passing Goldsworthy Junction on their way up to the ore mines for loading. The train comprised 312 100-ton capacity wagons and apart from the locos in the lead, two CM40-8Ms were positioned 104 wagons back, and another pair a further 104 wagons back. The total – seven locos with an impressive 31,000 horse power output to haul 30,000 tons of ore. That's what you call a train!

BHP CW60AC 6071 *Chichester* and SD40 3087 pass Goldsworthy Junction with a loaded ore train for Port Hedland. This was a 208 wagon train, which appeared to be the normal length of these trains.

The mid-train helpers were CM40-8M 5665 and SD40 3090. Note that both the SD40s are in the full BHPBIO scheme, reflecting the red earth, which with the blue sky made this Pom more than envious!

At the Highway 1 crossing outside Port Hedland, CM40-8M 5657 leads SD40s 3096 and 3082 with another load of iron ore for export.

BHP CM40-9M 5651 hauls a short ballast train bound for the siding at Bing WA. The ploughed earth necessitated a picture at the point outside Port Hedland to make a feature of the shot, April 2005.

2006

Queensland Rail 4005 and 4006 climb the bank past Callemondah shed and yards with a trainload of coal for export from the docks at Gladstone QLD. This was taken in February 2006 on my first visit to Queensland. Introduced in 1999 by Clyde EDI, these locos are fitted with EMD 710 diesels of 3,000HP/2,260kW and are classified JT42CU-AC.

QR 2304 and 2475 pass the same location with a train of cement wagons. The weather was not kind for photographs on this holiday – so what's new! The 2300s were built by Clyde in 1997, classed GTL22C- AC with a 645 EMD engine of 2,250HP/1,680kW, whilst 2475 was Clyde built in 1980 with a lower powered diesel of 1,500HP/1120kW and classed GL22C-2.

QR 4015 and 4021 are seen near Mount Larcom QLD with a train of coal hoppers from the Blackwater coal mine area heading for the docks at Gladstone in March 2006.

Electric locos 3550 and 3609 are seen heading in the opposite direction with coal hopper empties returning to the Blackwater area. These Bo-Bo-Bo locos were built by Walkers, with ASEA motors of 3,875HP/2,890kW introduced in 1986.

Classed CM30-8 and built by Goninan in 1995 with GE 7FDL diesel engines of 3,200HP/2,380kW, the 2800 class were noted for being the only double-cabbed GE locos in Australia. QR 2810 heads a short intermodal train southbound near Mount Larcom in February 2006.

In the older QR livery for these electric locos, 3544 and 3637 head south with another load of coal from the Blackwater mines for export from Gladstone. I was, by this time, on Mount Larcom station, having been kicked out from the previous location for being too close to the tracks, but the station is an ideal spot, with a track between the platform and virtually all the traffic, and a working toilet to boot!

This train had a pair of helpers mid-train, 3551 and 3520, complete with radio car for remote control from the lead loco. The locos show the old and new corporate colour schemes.

From the opposite direction Pacific National Queensland PN009 heads a Brisbane to Cairns intermodal, with the crossing bells ringing loudly in March 2006. This class is virtually the same as the QR 4000 class, that were introduced in 2004

Queensland Rail class F1A EMU set number 79 approaches Sunshine in the Brisbane suburbs, with a service from Ipswich to Caboolture in February 2006.

QR 2841 and 2185D (in the new QR National colours) pass Sunshine with a Brisbane-bound intermodal freight train. Queensland Rail 2185 is a GL26C-2 class loco built by Clyde in 1978 with an EMD 645 2,000HP/1,340kW diesel.

QR 2241D passes Sunshine with the Cairns to Brisbane Sunlander passenger service in February 2006. These are heavier versions of the 2300 class with similar power output.

The *City of Rockhampton* tilting EMU uses the bi-directional middle road at Sunshine with a Bundaberg to Brisbane service. Sunshine is certainly not living up to its title!

QR 2483D and 2321 pass Wacol QLD with an empty cattle train, which had been previously seen and smelled at Sunshine on its way to be unloaded at Redbank.

QR F1A class set number 82 arrives at Wacol with a Caboolture to Ipswich service in February 2006.

A CountryLink Explorer train, with power cars 2521 and 2507, arrives at Exeter NSW working from Canberra to Sydney in March 2006. The old English style signal box adds a pleasant feature to this little station.

Still in Australian National colours, EL55 leads sister loco EL63 in the CFCLA scheme with 6MB7 Melbourne to Brisbane intermodal at Towrang NSW in March 2006.

The difference in colours between Pacific National and FreightCorp is just about illustrated by 8166 and 8177, which head train 9339 from Port Kembla to Riverina grain empties, passing Towrang.

The sun is setting, but enough light is still available at Towrang to catch FreightCorp 8128, 48164 and 8169 working train 2122 Tarrago to Clyde rubbish service.

CFCLA 44204, repainted in an original colour scheme, Junee (ex-Austrac) 4836 and 4816, and CFCLA 44208, pass Goulburn NSW with train 9535 from Port Kembla to Riverina grain empties.

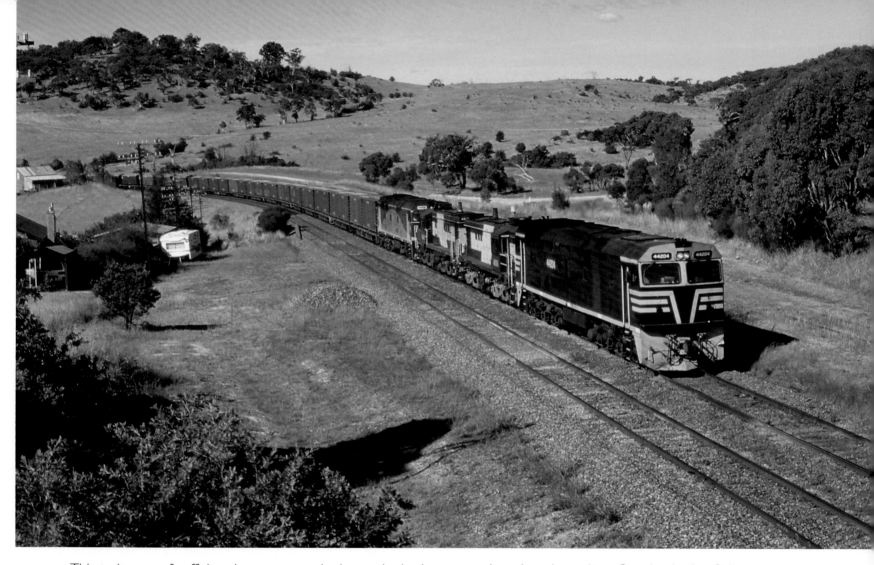

This train was of sufficient interest to make it worth chasing, so another view shows it at Gunning in the Cullerin ranges of New South Wales in March 2006.

In the new livery for the XPTs, CountryLink set 2004 passes East Maitland, in March 2006, on its way from Sydney to Murwillumbah NSW.

First sighting of the new era of Australian-built third generation locomotives, the C40aci introduced in 2005 by Goninan, fitted with GE 7FDL diesels of 4,000HP/3,000kW. Queensland Rail National 5008 and 5007 pass East Maitland in their striking new colours with coal empties returning from Newcastle to the Hunter Valley mining area.

MB4 Melbourne to Brisbane intermodal approaches Maitland behind a pair of NR class locos, 68 and 69. Both engines are still in National Rail colours, but carry Pacific National lettering. The front double diamond NR logo is scratched off.

A Newcastle-bound coal train leaves Maitland behind with new Pacific National 9034 at the head, supported by FreightCorp 8220 and 8250 in March 2006.

One of the New Millennium Sydney CityLink EMUs set M20 leaves Canterbury with a train from the city to Liverpool NSW in March 2006.

A pair of Alco DL500s, Southern Shorthaul 4483 and CFCLA 4471, pass Canterbury with a Port Botany-bound intermodal.

The driver of 4483, which is preserved by 3801 Ltd, sees me with camera and gives me a special eruption of the exhaust – thanks very much! The loco is hauling a coach and XPT power car, whence I have no idea.

Another Alco DL500, this one, 4461, owned by private company Lachlan Valley Railway, also heads for Port Botany with an intermodal train past Canterbury.

A westbound intermodal is headed by Silverton 442s3 coming out from under the road bridge at Canterbury station in March 2006. This is a standard 442 class of engine, but carries the unique style of numbering used by Silverton Transport.

2007

V Line N459 *City of Echuca* accelerates away from Kilmore East VIC on its way from Melbourne to Shepparton in February 2007. Dating from 1985, these EMD 645 2,250HP/1,680kW locos were built by Clyde. What more can you ask for than weather like this for taking train photos?!

The somersault signals add to the scene at Kilmore East, where a late-running Albury to Melbourne service heads away from the station behind V line N462 *City of Shepparton*.

A pair of what I regard as the best-looking 'Bubble Cars' stop at Kilmore East. V line 7016 and 7013 are working from Seymour to Melbourne.

V Line N461 *City of Ararat* stops at Kilmore East on its way from Melbourne to Shepparton. If you look closely, Kilmore seems to work to different hours than the rest of the world!

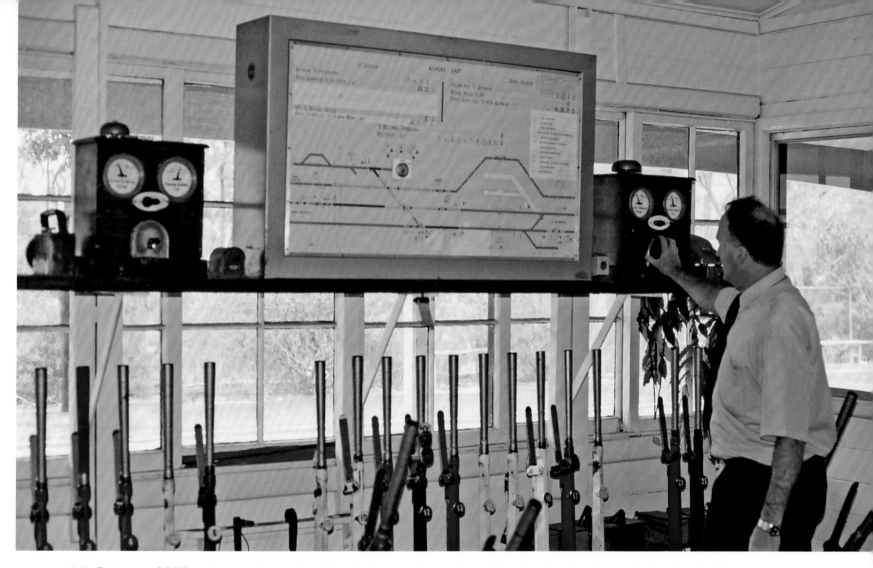

It is February 2007, and semaphore signalling is about to be replaced by electric signals, rendering the signal box at Kilmore East redundant. This view in the box brings back memories of the old days with the frame, track diagram and block instruments all visible.

Still in Freight Australia green but labelled for QR National, G534 and X54 pass Lightwood VIC with a rather short 1BM7 Brisbane to Melbourne intermodal.

FreightCorp 8153 and CFCLA GL111 pass Lightwood northbound with 3MC2 Melbourne to Griffith intermodal. One wonders what the man in the orange visi-vest between the telegraph poles is doing.

ARG CLP9 *Wiljakali* and Interail (ex-Northern Rivers) 42202 head towards Melbourne with 2SM9 intermodal from Sydney at Lightwood VIC.

Freight Australia liveried, now Pacific National A78, nears Lara VIC with a train of cement bound for North Geelong in February 2007.

A cloudy morning doesn't help to get the picture one seeks, but one does one's best; so here are Pac Nat A78 with H3, another A class and a G class with 9230 Tottenham to North Geelong approaching Lara.

Pac Nat ex-National Rail NR69 is seen near Lara with the Adelaide bound Overland of eight coaches.

It was a stroke of luck to find two Ghan liveried locos on the front of 4AB6 Adelaide to Brisbane intermodal, namely NR 78 and the unique AN3. They are seen having passed Lara on their way to Melbourne.

Adding to the colour variety, NR25 in Indian Pacific livery with NR 36 head west with 5MP4 intermodal from Melbourne to Perth, also seen at Lara in March 2007.

One of the former Pacific National X class, XRB 562, now rebuilt and acting as a cabless slave unit, is seen at Islington SA intermodal terminal partnered by NR 101. Note the sound baffles and the non-standard colour scheme.

Stabled on Dry Creek shed and restored to its original VR green and gold colours, C501 *George Brown* stands aloof in March 2007.

FreightLink FQ01 and ALF21 now re-lettered for Genesee & Wyoming Australia, pass Dry Creek with 6AD5 Adelaide to Darwin on a cloudy Saturday afternoon. The ALF class is almost identical to the G and BL classes. FQ01 is named *Kurra Kurraka*.

Three G&WA ALF class locos, 23, 24 and 22, head into Adelaide as they pass Dry Creek with an intermodal working from Darwin.

Looking very much cleaner than it did when seen in 2001, indigenous liveried NR52 passes Dry Creek with the Indian Pacific ex-Perth, bound for Sydney via Adelaide in March 2007.

2009

QR F5A EMU 166 stands in Roma Street station in Brisbane whilst working an Airport to Robina service in April 2009.

QR F1A EMU 85 comes to a halt at Caboolture QLD while working from Nambour to Roma Street with a selection of passengers waiting to board it. The camera kept trying to focus on those legs instead of the train!

In a distinctive colour scheme, QR F8B EMU 236 draws to a halt at Caboolture having travelled through from Ipswich via Brisbane.

Pacific National Queensland PN005 passes Caboolture on its way to Brisbane with an intermodal service from Cairns and Townsville, April 2009.

First sighting of the new V-Line livery, seen on N469 *City of Morwell,* which is working a Melbourne to Geelong train approaching Lara in April 2009.

V-locity DMU 1109 accelerates away from its stop at Lara on a service from Geelong to Melbourne.

Under a lowering sky, but caught by the late afternoon sun, V-Line A62 approaches Lara with a Melbourne to Warrnambool train in April 2009.

Not knowing that engineering work had blocked the broad gauge lines north of Craigieburn on this Saturday in April, I was in for some long waits to see trains. Having found a good location between there and Donnybrook, I arrived to see the tail of a train going south, and then waited three hours for the next train, 6AB6 Adelaide to Brisbane headed by Pacific National NRs 105, 76 and 86, seen negotiating a notable dip in the line. After another two hours with nothing on its way, I was so fed up, I took a photo of a tree, which looked like a witch! (see inset)

A special train hauled by preserved T356, owned by Steamrail, was running from Melbourne to Geelong, and was photographed passing Paisley VIC in April 2009.

Stabled in the yard at the old VR workshops at Newport in the outskirts of Melbourne, Pacific National S307 has not a blemish on it. It always seemed to me that putting the five air horns on top of the nose must obstruct the drivers view to some extent, but presumably the loading gauge didn't allow them to be put on the roof.

QR National 2819 has been fitted with standard gauge bogies in place of its normal 3'6'' sets, which it would have used in its home state. It is seen at West Swanston Dock in Melbourne.

A pair of SCT (Specialised Container Transport) G class locos, 533 and 511, are stabled at West Swanston Dock.

Stabled on Dynon Junction loco shed, NR 25 shows off the full splendour of the Indian Pacific colour scheme, but note that it does not carry any indication of its owner, Pacific National.

Interail 42206 carries the attractive livery of its previous owner Northern River. It is seen parked at North Dynon in April 2009.

T342 carries the striking colour scheme of its new owner, El Zoro, and is stabled on Dynon shed, Melbourne.

CFCLA use a wide variety of locomotive classes, S311 being an example as seen here on Dynon shed.

Pacific National XR555, rebuilt from a standard X class, looks rather shabby when seen on Dynon shed.

Another example of CFCLA's fleet is TL154, one of a class built in Australia and exported for use in Hong Kong. They were returned to Australia in 2005. This loco is also seen at Dynon shed. They were built by Clyde in 1955, with the EMD 567 diesel providing 1,300HP/980kW.

Why do people have to put a pole close up to a locomotive, and why do they park them next to poles?! Brand new LDP003 hardly has a mark on it as it stands in the sun on Dynon shed in April 2009. The loco is classed GT46C-Aca, introduced in 2007, with an EMD 710 diesel of 4,300HP/3,200kW. Although carrying QR National identification, it is leased from Downer Rail, LDP standing for Locomotive Demand Power.

SCT 008, 011 and 004 are nearly ready to leave the SCT facility at Laverton VIC, with 1MP9 Melbourne to Perth service comprised of the company's high cube wagons. Scotsmen would appreciate the king-sized thistles, but not up their kilts! These locos are of the same class as LDP003.

2011

A similar service is seen two years later, when SCT 011 and 012 pass Dry Creek on their way from Melbourne to Perth in March 2011.

Parked outside the EDI workshop at Dry Creek, FreightLink J class FJ04 carries the standard colour scheme devoid of over embellishment with aboriginal emblems.

Pacific National TT01, 04 and 03 approach Tarro station, NSW, with a full coal train bound for Newcastle area docks in March 2011. Another class identical with LDP003.

Having discharged its load, an empty coal train snakes round the station, avoiding line at Tarro behind Pac Nat 9003, 9015 and 9034.

In the early days of Xstrata Rail's own locomotives, four of them (normally three are used) head a train of empties passing Singleton NSW. The engines are XRN002, 009, 003 and 004, making a change from seeing the normal FreightCorp/Pacific National and QR National representatives. This class of locos have GE 7FDL engines of 4,350HP/3,250kW, and were built by United Group in 2010, typed C44aci.

QR National CLP12. 9 and 10 pass Beresfield one morning in March 2011 on their way with an intermodal service from Brisbane to Melbourne. The locos appear devoid of any ownership identification.

One of the three Whitehaven Coal class GT46C-Ace locomotives, WH002, is seen stabled at the EDI workshops at Kooragang Island at sunset in March 2011. The three locos owned by this company are GT46C Ace class as with SCT.

A very clean Pacific National TT104 heads two Whitehaven Coal locos, WH001 and WH003, with an empty coal train passing Beresfield. Just when I wanted the rear two engines to be in the lead!

A telescopic view from the footbridge at Beresfield station shows QR National 5004 and 5006 with a Newcastle-bound coal train being overtaken by CountryLink DMU 2002 working Telarah to Newcastle. The length of one of these coal trains is clearly demonstrated in this shot.

The new breed of DMUs, which have replaced the old 600 series units, is shown by 2705 starting off from Beresfield with a Newcastle to Telarah train.

The QR National 5020 class are a development of the earlier 5000 series, power being increased to 4,350HP/3,250kW from its 7FDL diesel. Classified C44acHi, 5029 and 5030 show off the new QRN corporate colour scheme as they head towards Newcastle with yet more coal passing Beresfield. They won't stay this clean for much longer! March 2011.

2012

When I made my first trip to Rockhampton QLD, in June 2012, the weather was, to say the least, appalling. But a shot had to be taken, so here are QR National 3546, 3557 and 3529 heading a Gladstone-bound Blackwater system coal train passing Rocklands South Junction. The train had mid-train helpers 3556 and 3567. My stay wasn't helped by being trapped on the top floor of the hotel for eighteen hours due to lift failure, so not a town with happy memories!

By the time I had moved up to the Mackay area, the weather had improved, enabling this shot of Pacific National 7108 and 7118 (with mid-train helper 7141), working a Goonyella system train of coal empties from Hay Point QLD passing Jilalan in June 2012. These 5,360HP/4,000kW locomotives were introduced by Siemens in Germany in 2007.

Passing the extensive workshops at Jilalan, QR National 3845 and 3741 (with mid-train helper 3760) head for Hay Point with a coal train. The 3800 series locos were also built by Siemens, but the 3700s were rebuilt in Australia from older QR electric locos, but using Siemens equipment.

QR National 4158 and 4164, in the new corporate colours, stand at Yukan QLD with a rake of four coal wagons in June 2012. These locos are similar to the 4000 class, but were introduced in 2007 with different electrical equipment.

QR 2470D and QR National 2477, in their respective colour schemes, approach Yukan with a short train of coal wagons. They returned shortly afterwards with more wagons, heading for Jilalan.

QR National 3817 and 3752 head a Hay Point-bound Goonyella system coal train near Yukan in the late morning of a day in June 2012.

Another coal train bound for Hay Point passes in the afternoon sunshine, hauled by QR National 3802 and 3757.

The full glory of the corporate Queensland Rail National colours are shown on a very clean 2199F, which is stabled at Mackay QLD in June 2012.

2014

Pacific National 8167, 48153 and 4898 cluster around the turntable at the loco shed at Werris Creek NSW in March 2014.

Stored for preservation (?) at Werris Creek, somewhat away from their previous areas of operation, were FreightCorp 8650 and 8501, with pantographs removed.

CountryLink DMUs 2505 and 2538 approach Werris Creek with a train from Sydney, which will split at the station — half destined for Tamworth, the other half for Armidale.

Typically grubby coal sector Pacific National locos TT114, 9209 and TT118 take the strain and open their throttles as they start the climb south out of Werris Creek yards with a Newcastle-bound coal train in March 2014.

A southbound coal train waits at Willow Creek NSW for the road to clear before starting the climb to the summit of the Liverpool ranges at Ardglen. The train is in the hands of Pacific National TT04, TT08 and TT108, all of the GT46C-Ace class, built by EDI Rail with EMD 710 diesel engines.

A train of coal empties descends the bank from Ardglen and passes the level crossing at Kankool behind Pacific National TT06, 9218 and TT05.

The morning mist hangs over the Dividing Range, as seen passing the end of the double track section from Ardglen. Pacific National 8166 and 8132 head north with a short train of grain empties.

The heat haze from the exhausts of Pacific National TT06, 9206 and TT05 indicate that they are working with throttles fully open as they slog past Kankool with another train load of coal for export from Kooragang Island at Newcastle.

The train seen waiting at Willow Creek has now almost reached the summit at Ardglen, at which point ...

... the three Pacific National bankers 8215, 8225 and 8226 will drop off and return to Kankool to rest before another exertion to the summit with the next coal train.

In a livery not unknown to a Pommie! Freightliner Powerhaul liveried CFCLA-owned CF4407 and 4408 have reached the summit at Ardglen with a Narrabri to Sydney train of containerised cotton. The hard work is now over. These C44 aci locos, with 4,250HP/3,170kW GE 7FDL diesels were introduced by United Group from 2008 for various operators, March 2014.

A northbound train of coal empties climbs away from Aberdeen NSW with Pacific National TT106, 9215 and TT105 doing the honours. The PN 9200 locos are of the same design as CFCLA's CF engines, April 2014.

Action takes place just south of Muswellbrook station NSW. Xstrata Rail XRN 017, 028 and 024 are parked with a short consist of coal wagons, whilst coming off the Ulan line is Pacific National 8248 with a train of concentrated mineral containers.

CFCLA VL 355 and GL109 head for the Ulan branch line at Muswellbrook with a train of empty mineral wagons. The safety markings near the platform edge are the best I have seen anywhere in the world. The design of the VL is one of the least attractive to my eyes, being built by a previous aircraft manufacturer, Avteq, at Sunshine, VIC, in 2001. They are fitted with EMD 645 engines of 3,000HP/2,240kW.

A coal train comes off the Ulan line at Muswellbrook station, behind CFCLA CF 4402, Pacific National 9208 and CFCLA CF 4404.

Pacific National TT06, 9205 and TT05 pull past Branxton station with northbound coal empties, with the train negotiating a noticeable dip where the line follows the contours of the land.

Pacific National 9017, 9007 and 9018 snake past the little station at Greta with a Newcastle-bound coal train.

With a smudge on the front end, Xstrata XRN 023, 014 and 016 come out from under the road bridge at Greta with northbound coal empties.

Variety at Lochinvar NSW, where to start off QR National 5031 and 5033 move gently along the additional track laid here to cope with the large increase in traffic. The coal train has probably come from the mines between Muswellbrook and Singleton. The new road bridge, which had to be built when the lines were widened, gives one of the best views for photography in the Hunter Valley in my opinion.

Pacific National BL30 and 8255 follow with a train of mineral concentrate containers.

Looking in the other direction, coal heads for Newcastle, and empties return behind CFCLA CF 4402, Pacific National 9208 and CFCLA CF 4404, which we saw previously at Muswellbrook with a coal train the previous day. The super modern station — all concrete and stainless steel — and the old Victorian era hotel make a superb contrast.

The fourth variety of loco owners and colour schemes to be seen at Lochinvar is demonstrated as Xstrata XRN 021, 029 and 018 pass by on the lightly used central track with more coal for export from Newcastle. The curves of the track layout help to make the picture. Lochinvar, April 2014.

CFCLA Freightliner Powerhaul CF 4408 and 4407 return north with a train of new container flats having been imported through Sydney and bound for Wee Waa NSW. The coal train has just cleared enough to get the photo at Medford NSW.

Xstrata XRN 023, 014 and 016 pass Medford with coal empties heading north. The lead loco still has the smudge on the front as when it was previously seen at Greta, April 2014.

The wires are ready for the new era of trains, as an Adelaide Metro train headed for Seacliff passes through Edwardstown SA with twin car DMU set 3108 leading ...

... and single car DMU 3024 at the rear. The overhead electrification portends things are going to change, April 2014.

The new CSR class, type SDA1, built in China, use German MTU engines of 4,000HP/3,000kW, and were built in 2012. Parked at the SCT facility at Bolivar SA, SBR (Specialised Bulk Rail) CSR 009 and SCT 006 sit in the sun in April 2014. The lead loco is named *Ziyang*. SBR is a subsidiary of SCT.